BROKEITIS

The #1 Disease Sweeping the Country and How to Stop Catching It

NOAH WAYAN

TOP ARTISTS 4U LLC

First Printing, 2025

ISBN

Paperback - 13: 978-1-968871-35-2

Ebook - 13: 978-1-968871-36-9

Top Artists 4 U LLC

15021 Ventura Blvd. #783 Sherman Oaks, CA 91403

TopArtists4U@gmail.com

Dedication

To everyone who's ever stared at their bank balance with a lump in their throat, swiped their card and whispered,

"Please go through,"

or stretched $5 like it was $500 - this book is for you. To the hustlers, the dreamers, the single parents, the nine-to-fivers, the side-giggers, and the people who refuse to give up - even when the math doesn't add up - this is your survival guide. And to the next generation: may you inherit wisdom instead of worry, freedom instead of fear, and wealth defined not just by dollars, but by peace of mind.

- Noah Wayan

INTRODUCTION

If you're reading this, chances are you've already caught it. Don't panic - it's not contagious through coughing or sneezing. It's much worse.

It's called **Brokeitis.**

Brokeitis (pronounced *broke-eye-tis*) is the number one disease sweeping the country. You won't see it trending on the news ticker. No doctor is going to hand you a prescription. But step into almost any home, office, or grocery store checkout line, and you'll see the symptoms everywhere.

The crazy part? Most people don't even know they have it. It sneaks in quietly, settles in deeply, and then one day you look around and realize your wallet has asthma, your bank account has high blood pressure, and your credit score is on life support.
So how do you know if you're infected? Let's run a quick self-test.

The Symptom Checklist (Warning: This Might Hurt)

- Do you check your bank app more often than you check your blood pressure?
- Have you ever prayed that a debit card swipe would just go through this one last time?
- Do you know the Taco Bell menu by heart because it's "cheap and filling"?
- Have you mastered the art of showering at the gym to save on your water bill?
- Do you keep your gas tank just above "E" and call it "budgeting"?
- Have you ever filled your fridge with condiments and bottled water because groceries were out of reach?
- Do you know the exact date your overdraft fee will hit - before the bank even reminds you?
- Have you ever celebrated payday only to realize half your check was gone before you left the parking lot?
- Do you say "I'm just window shopping" when really you're practicing self-control at its highest level?
- Have you ever debated whether Wi-Fi is a bill or a basic human right?
- Do you know which friend's house always has snacks - and find yourself "visiting" right before dinner?
- Have you ever stretched one pack of ramen into three meals and called it "meal prep"?
- Do you know the price of milk, gas, and eggs down to the penny but couldn't tell someone your own credit score?
- Have you ever carried an unpaid balance so long your credit card feels more like a roommate than a tool?
- Do you keep broken appliances because "one day I'll fix it," even though that day has been rescheduled since 2017?
- Have you ever filled your tank with $5 worth of gas just to "get by" until Friday?

- Do you keep clothes long past their expiration date because "it still works as a pajama shirt"?
- Have you ever attended a cookout with Tupperware ready because you knew that plate of leftovers was going to save your whole week?
- Do you borrow Netflix passwords like they're family heirlooms?
- Have you ever turned tap water into "detox water" just by slicing half a lemon and convincing yourself you're at a spa?

If you said yes to one - or worse, all of the above - you might be suffering from Brokeitis.

The Silent Spread

Unlike other illnesses, Brokeitis doesn't show up on X-rays or blood tests. You won't find it in a medical journal or hear about it at your annual checkup. But you *will* find it in the daily lives of millions of people doing everything "right" and still barely scraping by. Here's the bad news: Brokeitis is everywhere. Paycheck-to-paycheck workers have it. Government-check dependents have it.

Even folks with six-figure salaries aren't safe - because Brokeitis isn't just about income. It's about mindset, habits, and a system designed to keep you broke and buying. We joke about it. We laugh at memes that say, *"I'm so broke I can't even pay attention."* We shrug when friends say, *"Broke until payday!"* But underneath the jokes is real exhaustion, real stress, and real fear. Brokeitis is a silent pandemic. And the scariest part? **We've normalized it.**

Where Brokeitis Hides

You'll find Brokeitis in casual conversations:

"Man, I just got paid Friday and I'm already broke."

"Girl, I'm living off coffee and vibes until next week."

"Hey, can you spot me? I'll hit you back on payday."

You'll see it at work, when people bring lunch in old yogurt containers because eating out is out of reach. You'll hear it at church when the pastor says "tithes and offerings" and half the room checks their account balance mid-service.

You'll even find it on TikTok, where creators go viral showing "how to eat for $2 a day" or "how to survive until Friday with $13 and a half-tank of gas."Brokeitis hides in break rooms, carpool conversations, and grocery checkout lines. It's in the sighs when the register total pops up higher than expected, in the smiles that hide stress when someone says, *"Let's split the bill evenly."*
It's everywhere.

The Emotional Toll

Brokeitis isn't just about numbers in a bank account - it's about what it does to your soul. It makes you feel like you're failing, even when you're working harder than ever. It eats at your confidence when you can't afford what others seem to buy without blinking. It creates shame that keeps you quiet instead of asking for help. It sneaks into marriages when couples fight over money more than love. It sneaks into friendships when you dodge social events because

"I can't afford it."

It even sneaks into parenting, when you feel guilty for not being able to give your kids what other children have. And the stress? It doesn't just sit in your mind - it shows up in your body. Headaches, sleepless nights, tight shoulders, upset stomachs. Your body keeps the score of Brokeitis.

How the System Feeds It

Here's the kicker: Brokeitis thrives because the system wants it to. Prices rise while wages crawl. Banks charge overdraft fees for the crime of already being broke. Credit card companies dangle "rewards" while trapping people in cycles of debt. Advertising convinces you that your worth is tied to what you own, not who you are. From "buy now, pay later" apps to payday loans to $8 coffees that promise confidence in a cup, the culture is designed to keep us consuming - even when we can't afford it. Brokeitis doesn't just live in us; it's fed by everything around us.

My Story (Proof That It's Real)

I know Brokeitis because I lived it. I've been the guy eating fast food not because I loved it, but because it was cheaper than buying real groceries. I've been the person praying my car wouldn't break down because the repair bill would've been the end of me. I've been the one lying awake at night, wondering if my car might double as both transportation and a bedroom.

I've made choices that money "experts" would shake their heads at. I've bought things I couldn't afford, paid bills late, and lived with the anxiety that maybe this was just the way life was always going to be. And yet - I found my way out. Not through a lottery ticket or a rich uncle, but through small shifts, new habits, and knowledge I wish I'd been taught years ago. That's what this book is about.

The Good News: Brokeitis Can Be Cured

Brokeitis might be widespread, but it isn't terminal. You don't have to stay broke. You don't have to keep repeating the cycle. There is a cure - but it doesn't come in the form of quick fixes or "get rich overnight" scams. The cure starts with awareness. It grows with new habits. And it becomes permanent when you learn to see money differently - not as something you're constantly chasing, but as something you can direct with confidence. This book is not a finance textbook.

I'm not going to bury you in charts, formulas, or jargon. This is a survival guide, a social critique, and sometimes a comedy sketch. We're going to laugh at the ridiculousness of it all, cry at the truth of it, and most importantly -nfind a way out together.

What to Expect

In the chapters ahead, I'll break down the symptoms, the root causes, the types, and - most importantly - the cure. Along the way, I'll share stories that are funny, frustrating, and painfully true. We'll talk about how society has trained us to consume more than we need, waste more than we use, and ignore problems until they knock on the front door. We'll confront uncomfortable truths but also uncover powerful solutions. If you've ever been broke - or felt like you were one bill away from disaster - you'll find yourself in these pages.

Final Word Before We Begin

So here's the deal: Brokeitis is real. It's everywhere. And if you've read this far, you probably already know you've got a touch of it. But that's okay. Because recognizing it is the first step to healing it. This isn't going to be a TED Talk. It's not going to be a boring lecture. It's an SOS, a survival kit, and a little bit of group therapy for anyone who's tired of living in the shadow of being broke. So buckle up.

Laugh if you need to. Cry if you must. But whatever you do, don't look away. Because the cure is closer than you think. Brokeitis is real. It's curable. And together, we're going to break the cycle.

1

WHAT IS BROKEITIS?

Most people think being broke and having Brokeitis are the same thing. They're not. Being broke is temporary - it's a moment, a situation, a season you pass through. Brokeitis, on the other hand, is a lifestyle. It's when being broke isn't just where your money is - it's where your mindset is.

Think of it this way:

- **Broke** is when your car payment is late this month.
- **Brokeitis** is when late payments are so normal that the repo man waves at you like an old neighbor.

Being broke is catching a cold. Brokeitis is walking around with pneumonia and convincing yourself it's just "allergies."

Circumstances vs. Choices

Brokeitis is a disease of both circumstance *and* choice. Sometimes you catch it because of life: layoffs, medical bills, the rent increase your landlord hit you with out of nowhere. Maybe your car broke down the same week your kid needed braces. Life has a way of stacking bills higher than your paycheck. But other times? You catch it because of habits.

Buying sneakers you can't afford. Eating out instead of cooking. Flexing on Instagram with a vacation you haven't actually paid for - while Sallie Mae is still leaving voicemails like a clingy ex. Brokeitis is sneaky. It doesn't show up in a blood test, but it does show up in your Amazon order history, your DoorDash receipts, and your "insufficient funds" alerts at 2:00 a.m.

How Brokeitis Spreads

Like any epidemic, Brokeitis spreads fast. And the transmission methods? They're everywhere. **It spreads through comparison.** Your neighbor gets a new SUV and suddenly your perfectly fine car looks like it belongs in a museum exhibit called *The Struggle Years.* **It spreads through culture.** Advertisers whisper, "You're not enough unless you buy this." Influencers post their "unboxing" videos and make you feel like you're failing life because you don't have the latest gadget, skincare routine, or limited-edition hoodie.

It spreads through bad education. Let's be real - schools taught us how to dissect frogs but not how to balance a checkbook. Nobody explained interest rates or compound debt, but we sure know the Pythagorean theorem. **It spreads through desperation.** That one payday loan you swore you'd pay back in two weeks? Yeah, it turned into a three-year relationship. That "buy now, pay later" plan? You definitely bought now, but the paying later is killing you softly. And once it's in your system, it shows up everywhere:

- In the way you spend more on takeout than groceries.
- In the way you sign up for five streaming services but can't remember the password to any of them.

- In the way you treat credit cards like Monopoly money, reassuring yourself, *"Future me will figure it out."*

Why It's Not Just About Money

Here's the real kicker: Brokeitis isn't only about having less money - it's about having less peace. Money stress doesn't stay in your wallet. It moves into your body. It makes you tired, anxious, irritable. It keeps you awake at night doing math in your head:

> ***"If the electric bill is $112 and I move $30 from savings, then…oh wait, I don't have savings."***

It sneaks into marriages when couples stop talking about love and start fighting about bills. It sneaks into friendships when you dodge invitations because "I can't afford it." It sneaks into parenting when your kid asks for something small and you have to say no - not because it's bad for them, but because it's bad for your bank account. So yes, Brokeitis is about dollars - but it's also about dignity, stability, and sanity.

The Meme Economy of Brokeitis

One of the most dangerous things about Brokeitis is how we've turned it into entertainment. We make memes about overdraft fees. We laugh at TikToks where people say, "I checked my account and I got $4.17 to last me until payday." We've made being broke a personality trait, like being the "funny friend" or the "gym rat." But while we laugh, the stress is eating us alive. Jokes might lighten the load for a moment, but they don't pay the bills. And the more we normalize it, the less urgent it feels to fix it. Imagine if we did this with any other illness:

- "Haha, I got the flu again. Hashtag flu life."
- "Woke up with pneumonia, but at least I'm still cute."
- "Diabetes gang, where you at?"

Ridiculous, right? Yet with Brokeitis, we shrug and laugh and move on - until the debt collectors start calling, the eviction notice shows up, or the repo truck backs into the driveway.

Broke vs. Brokeitis

Let's break it down even simpler:

- **Broke** is when you say, "I can't go out this weekend, I'm tight on cash."
- **Brokeitis** is when you say, "I can't go out this weekend, this month, or maybe this year."
- **Broke** is skipping Starbucks for a week to save money.
- **Brokeitis** is convincing yourself that caffeine withdrawal is just part of adulthood.
- **Broke** is a season.
- **Brokeitis** is a cycle.

Broke is a flat tire. Brokeitis is driving on the rim for six months, telling yourself, *"As long as I don't go over 40 mph, I'll be fine."*

What Brokeitis Feels Like

If you've never experienced it (and I doubt that), here's what it feels like:

- Payday feels like Christmas morning, but by Tuesday you're already counting pennies.
- You avoid unknown phone numbers because 50% of them are bill collectors and the other 50% are "special offers" you can't afford.
- You open your mail over the trash can because most of it is bills, final notices, or credit card offers you're too scared to accept but too broke to ignore.

- You know the exact time your direct deposit hits, down to the minute.

Brokeitis isn't just being broke - it's being broke in high definition. It's a soundtrack of overdraft alerts, a calendar full of due dates, and a mood board of "someday I'll get ahead."

The Long-Term Effects

Left untreated, Brokeitis mutates.

- **Financially**, it locks you into cycles of debt that feel impossible to escape. You pay interest on top of interest, until you realize you've bought the same couch three times over and it's still not fully paid.
- **Emotionally**, it makes you feel small. You start believing you'll never have enough, never get ahead, never breathe easy.
- **Socially**, it isolates you. You dodge weddings, birthdays, or vacations because "I can't swing it." Before long, you're lonely - not because you don't want to show up, but because your wallet won't let you.
- **Generationally**, it passes down. Kids raised in Brokeitis households absorb the fear, the scarcity, the shame. They learn money is stress, not security.

Why You Need to Pay Attention

The problem isn't just that Brokeitis exists - it's that too many people treat it like a joke until it takes over their lives. We laugh at it. We normalize it. We hide it. Meanwhile, it's eating away at our futures. If you don't recognize Brokeitis and deal with it, it grows. It spreads. It passes on to your kids. It locks you into a future of always hustling, never resting, and never feeling secure. It makes life about survival instead of living. But here's the truth: Brokeitis is not a life sentence. You can cure it. The first step? Admit you've got it. And by the time you finish this book, you'll know not only that you have it - you'll also know how to fight back.

Closing Thought

Brokeitis is bigger than bills. It's bigger than being broke. It's a way of thinking, a way of living, and a system designed to keep you stuck. But once you see it, you can't unsee it. And once you admit it, you can begin to fight it. The rest of this book is your prescription. So let's get to work.

2

THE SYMPTOMS WE IGNORE

The thing about Brokeitis is this: most people don't even realize they have it. Or, they realize it but laugh it off like it's no big deal. We treat money struggles like allergies in spring - annoying, but normal. But here's the problem: Brokeitis symptoms don't go away with a couple of allergy pills. Ignore them long enough, and they'll eat away at your health, your relationships, and your future. So let's get real. Here are some of the most common symptoms of Brokeitis that we've all seen - and probably lived.

1. The Bank-App Anxiety Shuffle

You know you have Brokeitis when you check your bank balance like you're checking the weather forecast. You're not excited to see sunshine - you're just praying there's no storm. And let's be honest, we've all done that move where you slide your debit card and look away from the screen, whispering, *"Please, Lord, just this one time."* That split second feels like waiting on medical test results. *Positive or negative? Am I good or doomed?* The craziest part? You already know what the account says. You just can't stop yourself from checking.

People with Brokeitis treat their bank app like toxic relationships - you know it's going to hurt, but you keep going back anyway.

2. Fast-Food Fine Dining

If the cashier at Taco Bell, McDonald's, or Wendy's knows your order before you say it, you might be dealing with Brokeitis. Cheap calories feel like a financial win—until your health and waistline send you another kind of bill. Fast food becomes survival, not choice. You convince yourself, *"It's only five bucks, cheaper than groceries."* But five bucks here, seven bucks there, and suddenly you've dropped hundreds in a month - money that could've covered real meals. It's not that you don't want fresh food. It's that fresh food feels like luxury. Brokeitis makes the dollar menu your dietitian.

3. Gym Membership = Utilities Plan

Some people go to the gym to get fit. People with Brokeitis go to the gym to get clean. A workout? Optional. A hot shower that doesn't raise your water bill? Priceless. I knew someone who used Planet Fitness like a spa membership. He didn't lift weights, didn't run the treadmill - he walked in, showered, brushed his teeth in the sink, grabbed the free Tootsie Rolls, and left. Brokeitis turns gyms into part of your utilities plan: $10 a month for running water, climate control, and, if you're bold, a nap in the massage chair.

4. Gas Tank Limbo

If you've ever driven with your gas light on so long it feels like a permanent dashboard feature, welcome to the club. The game is called *"How Far Can I Stretch This $5?"* Spoiler alert: nobody ever wins. You learn the quirks of your car like a survivalist. *"I can make it 17 more miles before it actually dies."* You start praying at stoplights, coasting downhill, and swearing you'll "fill up next time." But next time never comes. Brokeitis makes every trip a gamble: groceries or gas? Drive to work or risk remote "sick days" because the tank's dry?

5. Payday Paradox

Payday is supposed to be exciting. For people with Brokeitis, it's depressing - because the money is already gone before it even lands. Bills, debts, and that "treat yourself" impulse tag-team your paycheck into submission before you can blink. You log into your account, see the deposit, and then - poof - it evaporates into rent, car notes, and overdue payments. Payday doesn't feel like a blessing. It feels like a brief visit from money before it packs its bags and leaves again.

6. The Fridge of Shame

You open the fridge and it looks like a condiment museum: ketchup, mustard, maybe some pickles - but no actual food. Milk? Expired. Eggs? Gone. Vegetables? What are those? It's not that you don't want food - it's that real groceries cost upfront money Brokeitis doesn't allow. Condiments become meals. Mayonnaise sandwiches. Hot sauce on crackers. Or the classic: a cold slice of American cheese rolled up like sushi. The fridge becomes a reminder of scarcity. You don't even bother grocery shopping with a list anymore - you shop with vibes and prayers.

7. The Wi-Fi Debate

Brokeitis convinces you to have deep philosophical conversations like: *"Is Wi-Fi a bill... or a basic human right?"* You'll sacrifice cable, you'll juggle credit cards, but internet? That feels non-negotiable. When the Wi-Fi cuts off, it's like losing oxygen. Your job applications, your streaming "escape," even your kids' homework depend on it. And so you'll pay the Wi-Fi bill late, stack late fees, beg the company for extensions - because in 2025, no internet means no survival.

8. Ramen Gourmet

Stretching one pack of ramen into three meals is not meal prep, my friend. It's survival mode. People with Brokeitis know every way to "upgrade" ramen: hot sauce, frozen peas, maybe an egg if you're lucky. You even convince yourself you're being creative. "It's like Top Chef… but broke." But behind the jokes is the truth: your body can't thrive on sodium and starch. Brokeitis doesn't just rob your wallet - it robs your health.

9. The Social Media Flex

Brokeitis isn't just about money - it's about appearances. You might be broke, but on Instagram? You're living your "best life." New selfies, staged coffee cups, maybe even a vacation pic (even though you'll be paying that trip off for the next two years). It's not always vanity - it's survival. Brokeitis tells you, *"If you look successful, maybe no one will notice you're struggling."* But flexing for the 'Gram while drowning in debt is like putting fresh paint on a collapsing house. Pretty on the outside. Crumbling on the inside.

10. Relationship Stress Test

Money fights are one of the top reasons relationships fall apart. With Brokeitis, every date night, bill split, or grocery run can turn into a full-blown argument. *"Why'd you buy that?"* becomes the new *"I love you."* Brokeitis sneaks into romance and replaces affection with suspicion. Instead of planning futures, you're arguing about past purchases. Instead of intimacy, you're drowning in tension. Love can survive a lot. But constant financial stress? That's a heavy load for even the strongest relationships.

Why We Ignore the Symptoms

Here's the saddest part: most people don't take these symptoms seriously until things get really bad - eviction, repossession, homelessness. Until then, it's memes and jokes about "being broke but still cute." We laugh at Brokeitis because it's easier than facing it. But ignoring the symptoms doesn't cure the disease. In fact, it makes it worse. And here's the truth nobody wants to say: Brokeitis thrives in silence. The less we talk about money, the more power it has over us.

The Wake-Up Call

If any of these symptoms hit a little too close to home, don't feel ashamed. The purpose here isn't guilt - it's awareness. Brokeitis is a shared struggle. Millions live it daily. But the first step to breaking it is recognizing it. Because the first step in curing Brokeitis is admitting you've got it.

3

THE ROOT CAUSE OF BROKEITIS

Every disease has a root cause. The flu? A virus. Heart disease? Diet, stress, genetics. Brokeitis? That's a little trickier. It doesn't come from germs, but from habits, culture, and a system that profits off keeping you broke. If we're being honest, most people didn't "wake up one day" with Brokeitis. It crept in slowly, one bad money choice at a time, one cultural lie at a time, one financial system loophole at a time. Before you know it, you're coughing up overdraft fees and sneezing out late notices. Let's break it down.

1. Eating the Fruit Before You Plant the Tree

One of the biggest root causes of Brokeitis is impatience. We want the rewards before we put in the work. We buy cars we can't afford. We swipe credit cards for vacations we haven't earned. We live in houses that stretch our budgets like old rubber bands. Instead of planting the tree - saving, investing, building stability - we try to enjoy the fruit first. And when the fruit runs out? We wonder why we're still hungry. It's like planting an apple seed today and then staring at the dirt tomorrow, wondering why there's no pie yet. The tree takes time.

The roots need to grow before the fruit can come. But in a world of next-day shipping and instant gratification, who wants to wait? I remember a friend of mine who financed a brand-new luxury car while working a job that barely covered rent. He was shining on the outside, broke on the inside. That car smelled like leather, but it also smelled like debt. Within a year, the repo man had reclaimed his ride, and he was back on the bus—this time with an extra side of embarrassment. Brokeitis thrives in impatience. It convinces us that appearances today matter more than security tomorrow.

2. They Took My Piece of the Pie

Another cause is lack of knowledge. If you don't know how money works, it will work against you. And trust me, there are plenty of institutions that profit off keeping you in the dark.
Banks. Credit card companies. Lenders. Retailers. They all know one thing: your ignorance is their income. Think about it:

- How many of us were taught in school how to budget, build credit, or invest?
- How many of us learned about APRs, interest, or taxes the hard way?
- How many of us signed up for "free" credit cards in college and ended up paying for those mistakes a decade later?

I still remember standing at a college fair, lured in by the promise of a free T-shirt if I signed up for a credit card. I thought I was winning. I got the T-shirt, all right - but I also got a debt cycle that haunted me for years. That shirt is long gone. The interest payments? Those stuck around. The truth is simple: if you don't know, you don't know. And Brokeitis thrives in that blind spot.

---

3. The Consumerism Trap

Our society runs on one fuel: spend, spend, spend. Everywhere you look, someone is telling you that you need more.

- Ads whisper, "You're not enough until you buy this."
- Social media shows you people "living better" than you - even though half of them are just as broke.
- Holidays aren't about family anymore - they're about buying, upgrading, flexing.

We're trained to believe happiness lives in a shopping cart. And when we can't afford it, we swipe plastic or borrow money to "keep up." Brokeitis loves consumerism because it disguises itself as normal life. Everyone's doing it. Everyone's upgrading. Everyone's buying. So when you do it too, it doesn't feel reckless - it feels responsible.

"Of course I need the newest phone. Everyone else has one."

But here's the dirty secret: half the people showing off their "blessings" online are just as broke as you. They've just mastered the art of looking rich while drowning in debt.

4. Hand-Me-Down Habits

Brokeitis is often generational. Kids grow up watching their parents struggle with money and inherit the same habits. If Mom and Dad never saved, odds are you won't either. If money was a constant fight in your household, you might grow up fearing it instead of managing it. If your family lived paycheck to paycheck, "normal" for you may always look like survival instead of stability. I once asked a group of adults how many of them had heard the phrase "Money doesn't grow on trees" growing up.

Almost every hand went up. Now here's the kicker - nobody followed that up with, "So here's how to actually grow money." The conversation stopped at *scarcity*, never moved toward *strategy*. So we learned money is stressful, mysterious, and scarce. And we carried those hand-me-down habits into adulthood, passing them on like unwanted family heirlooms. The cycle continues until someone breaks it - but breaking it takes awareness, courage, and new knowledge.

5. Mistaking Wants for Needs

Here's another sneaky root cause: not knowing the difference between what we want and what we need. Do you really need the newest iPhone, or just want it? Do you really need to order takeout tonight, or could you cook? Do you really need all those subscriptions (Netflix, Hulu, Disney+, Prime, HBO Max, Apple TV…), or could you live with one? We confuse comfort with necessity.

Brokeitis feeds on that confusion. There's nothing wrong with wanting nice things. The problem is when wants consistently outrun needs. That's when Brokeitis moves in, packs a suitcase, and makes itself at home. One of my friends used to say, "I can't live without my Starbucks." Really? You can't live without a latte? Water is free, but apparently survival now costs $6. Brokeitis has a way of convincing us that luxuries are lifelines.

6. Silence Around Money

Finally, one of the deepest causes: nobody talks about money honestly. We brag when we're doing well, hide when we're not, and avoid the topic altogether in families, friendships, and schools. That silence breeds ignorance, shame, and repeated mistakes. Think about how taboo money is in conversation. You can ask people about their love lives, their politics, even their medical history before you can ask them how much money they make. That silence isn't harmless - it's deadly. When we don't talk about money, we don't learn about it. We repeat the same mistakes our parents made. We make financial decisions in isolation, embarrassed to ask for help. Brokeitis thrives in silence because silence keeps us stuck.

The Truth About Brokeitis

Brokeitis doesn't just come from being broke. It comes from:

- Lack of financial education.
- Bad habits reinforced by culture.
- A system designed to keep you consuming instead of saving.
- A silence around money that keeps us trapped in cycles.

And here's the kicker: until you dig out the root, the disease keeps coming back. You can patch it with payday loans, side hustles, or "budget hacks," but unless you deal with the underlying cause, Brokeitis will always find its way back into your life. It's like cutting weeds without pulling the roots - they'll grow back stronger.

So What Now?

If you've been wondering, "Why does this keep happening to me?" - now you know. It's not just bad luck. It's not just one bad decision. It's a system, a mindset, and a cycle. But here's the hope: once you know the cause, you can treat it. Because Brokeitis, just like any other disease, doesn't have to be permanent.

4

THE HIDDEN COSTS OF BROKEITIS

We've laughed at the symptoms. We've pointed out the types. But here's the thing about Brokeitis: underneath the jokes, the memes, and the "relatable struggles" is something far more dangerous. Brokeitis doesn't just take money out of your wallet. It takes pieces of your health, your relationships, and your peace of mind. It's not just a financial disease - it's an emotional and physical one, too. Most people don't connect the dots. They see the overdraft fees, the empty fridge, the gas tank on "E." What they don't see is how those things add up to stress, anxiety, shame, and broken trust. That's the hidden cost. And sometimes, it's a price far greater than the one on your bills.

Stress: The Silent Side Effect

Money stress is one of the most powerful stressors in modern life. In fact, countless studies show that financial worries consistently rank as the **number one cause of stress** - higher than work, higher than health, higher even than family drama.And stress doesn't stay in your head. It shows up in your body. It looks like:

- Sleepless nights spent doing math in your head that never quite adds up.
- Tight shoulders and headaches that creep in every time you see a bill in the mailbox.
- Anxiety that makes your heart race every time your phone buzzes, wondering if it's a debt collector.

I remember when I was deep in my own Brokeitis, my chest would tighten every time I saw a letter with a windowed envelope. You know the kind - official, unforgiving. My body reacted before my mind even processed it. That's how deeply stress burrows in. Brokeitis doesn't just drain your bank account—it literally drains your health.

Anxiety and Shame: The Invisible Burden

Brokeitis doesn't just live in the numbers. It lives in the emotions we carry silently. It looks like embarrassment when your card declines in public. It looks like dodging phone calls from numbers you don't recognize. It looks like forcing a smile when friends ask you to go out, while inside you're panicking about how to say no without sounding broke. And here's the worst part: we don't talk about it. We bottle it up. Instead of admitting, *"I'm struggling,"* we laugh it off:

> ***"I'm broke but still cute!"***

Humor becomes the mask for shame. But shame is heavy. It makes you feel small. It convinces you that money struggles are a reflection of your worth, instead of just your current circumstances. And left unchecked, that shame becomes silence. You don't ask for help. You don't open up. You just carry it like a secret weight.

Relationships on the Line

If money stress is heavy alone, it's even heavier when two people are carrying it together. Or worse - arguing about who should carry more. Money fights are one of the leading causes of divorce. Couples who love each other deeply can still get torn apart by Brokeitis. It sneaks into conversations like an uninvited guest.

> **"Why did you buy that?" replaces "How was your day?"**

> **"We can't afford this" replaces "I love you."**

Silent resentment grows where laughter used to live. I've seen couples split not because they didn't love each other, but because they couldn't survive the pressure of bills, debt, and constant financial uncertainty. Brokeitis doesn't just attack wallets - it attacks intimacy. And it's not just romantic relationships. Friendships take hits, too. When you can't afford to go out, you start saying no. At first, your friends understand. But eventually, the distance grows. You're not at the dinners, not at the trips, not at the celebrations. One day you realize you're not just broke - you're lonely. Brokeitis isolates. It doesn't just cut you off from opportunities. It cuts you off from people.

Parenting with Brokeitis

Perhaps one of the most heartbreaking hidden costs of Brokeitis shows up in parenting. When your child asks for something simple - a field trip fee, a pair of shoes, an ice cream after school - and you can't provide it, the guilt is crushing. You want to give them the world, but Brokeitis has you locked in survival mode. Kids notice more than we think. They hear the whispered arguments. They see the bills on the table.

They feel the tension when money is tight. And without meaning to, we pass Brokeitis down like a family heirloom. Generational Brokeitis doesn't just come from lack of money. It comes from the emotional imprint of growing up in scarcity. Children raised in Brokeitis households often inherit the same fears, the same shame, the same silence. That's how the cycle continues.

The Health Toll

Stress. Anxiety. Guilt. All of these pile up, but the body eventually sends the bill. Brokeitis has been linked (directly or indirectly) to:

- High blood pressure.
- Heart disease.
- Depression and anxiety disorders.
- Insomnia.
- Weight gain or unhealthy weight loss (depending on coping habits).

Think about it: if you're constantly eating cheap fast food because that's all you can afford, your body pays. If you're losing sleep worrying about bills, your immune system weakens. If you're under constant stress, your body is in fight-or-flight mode all the time - burning energy, spiking cortisol, wearing down your health. It's not an exaggeration to say Brokeitis can literally shave years off your life.

The Illusion of Escape

Another hidden cost of Brokeitis is the constant temptation to escape. When life feels overwhelming, distractions become survival tools. Streaming, scrolling, shopping - even things like gambling or drinking - can feel like relief. But these escapes often deepen the problem. You spend more money trying to forget that you don't have money. You numb the stress instead of solving it. And the next morning, the bills are still there - only now you feel worse. Brokeitis doesn't just trap your wallet. It traps your mind in cycles of avoidance.

Why We Don't See It

If Brokeitis is this damaging, why don't more people talk about it? Why don't we treat it like the crisis it is? Because we've normalized it. We joke about being broke. We meme our way through overdraft fees. We trade war stories about surviving until payday. It's easier to laugh than to face the truth. But ignoring the hidden costs doesn't make them go away. It just lets them grow stronger.

The Real Price of Brokeitis

The real price of Brokeitis isn't just late fees or debt. It's:

- The friendships that quietly fade away.
- The marriages that crack under pressure.
- The parents who carry guilt like a second mortgage.
- The health problems that pile up silently until they're too loud to ignore.
- The dreams that die quietly in the corner because survival stole the energy to chase them.

This is why Brokeitis is so deadly. Because it convinces you the only thing at stake is money, when really, *everything* is at stake.

A Hard Truth and a Soft Landing

Here's the hard truth: Brokeitis is costing you more than you think. Not just in dollars, but in life. But here's the soft landing: once you see it, you can change it. Once you name it, you can face it. Awareness is the first step. And this chapter is about opening your eyes. Because you deserve more than survival. You deserve health, love, peace, and stability. And none of that is possible if Brokeitis is running your life unchecked.

Closing Reflection

The hidden costs of Brokeitis are real. They're heavy. They hurt. But facing them is the only way to start healing. You've laughed at the symptoms. You've recognized the root causes. Now you've seen the damage Brokeitis really does. The next step? Diagnosis. That's where we'll turn next. Because Brokeitis wears many masks, and the only way to cure it is to know exactly which one you're dealing with.

5

LESSONS FROM ROCK BOTTOM

Nobody signs up to hit rock bottom. It's not on anyone's vision board. You don't see people writing *"live in my car"* under their five-year goals. But life has a funny way of taking you there whether you planned it or not. And here's the truth: as much as it hurts, rock bottom can be the best classroom you'll ever sit in. When you're stripped down to nothing, you start seeing things clearly. No more pretending, no more flexing, no more distractions. Just you, your reality, and the raw lessons staring you in the face.

A Scene at the Bottom

Picture this: You're standing at the checkout line with a basket of groceries - milk, eggs, bread, maybe a box of cereal for the kids. You pull out your debit card, swipe, and wait. Declined. You try again, knowing in your gut it won't work, but hoping for a miracle. Declined. The cashier gives you that polite-but-pitying look. The people behind you shuffle impatiently. And there you are, deciding what to put back so the total drops low enough to scrape by. That's rock bottom. It's humiliating. It's heavy. But it's also clarifying. Because in that moment, you realize something has to change.

The Humility Lesson

When you're at rock bottom, pride goes out the window real fast. Suddenly, things you once looked down on don't seem so bad.

- You might find yourself waiting in line at a food pantry.
- You might be rolling coins to buy groceries.
- You might be digging through the closet to sell clothes just to pay a bill.

It's humbling. But humility is powerful - because it strips away the illusion that you've "got it all together" and forces you to get real. A friend of mine once told me, "The day I applied for food stamps was the day I swallowed my pride. But it was also the day I started climbing out, because I stopped caring what people thought and started caring about what I needed to do." Humility doesn't feel good, but it's a reset button. It shifts your perspective from appearances to survival, and eventually, to growth.

The Creativity Lesson

Rock bottom makes you resourceful. You start finding ways to stretch a dollar until it screams.

- That $5 gas tank challenge? You've mastered it.
- Ramen noodles? You've turned them into a five-course meal.
- Furniture? You're suddenly a pro at Craigslist, yard sales, and making hand-me-downs look brand new.

I once knew a guy who built an entire living room set out of wooden pallets he found behind stores. Was it fancy? No. Did it work? Absolutely. That kind of creativity doesn't come from Pinterest - it comes from necessity. And here's the beauty: once you climb out of rock bottom, that creativity doesn't leave you. It becomes one of your greatest strengths. You learn to see opportunities where others see obstacles. You learn to make a way when there seems to be none.

The Compassion Lesson

When you've been down, you stop judging others who are there. You stop saying, *"I'd never let myself get like that,"* because you already did. You stop assuming homelessness equals laziness. You stop believing poverty equals stupidity. Rock bottom has a way of softening your heart. Suddenly, the person asking for change on the street corner isn't invisible anymore. You see them. You recognize something in their eyes, because you've felt it too. That compassion? That's humanity at work. And it sticks with you. Even years later, when you've climbed out, you don't forget. You give more. You judge less. You understand on a level that only lived experience can teach.

The Reality Check Lesson

Here's one of the hardest truths: most people don't take problems seriously until they land at their doorstep. You can watch the news, read the stats, scroll the memes - but nothing wakes you up like losing your home, your job, or your health. Brokeitis feels far away until the eviction notice has your name on it. Then suddenly, it's not funny anymore. It's urgent. Reality checks come in many forms:

- A car repossessed while you're still inside the grocery store.
- A landlord changing the locks on your apartment.
- A medical bill bigger than your savings account.

Rock bottom is the alarm clock that you can't snooze. It's harsh, it's disruptive, but it's also what forces you to take action you might've avoided otherwise.

The Rebuild Lesson

The final lesson rock bottom teaches is this: once you've lost everything, you realize what really matters. And it's not stuff.

- It's peace.
- It's security.
- It's freedom.
- It's knowing that you'll be okay even if the world shakes again.

When you've had to start over from nothing, you learn to build differently. You stop using cheap materials - quick fixes, bad habits, appearances. You start laying bricks of discipline, patience, education, and resilience. Rock bottom strips you down so you can rebuild with stronger materials. It takes away the flimsy stuff so you can create a foundation that lasts.

A Personal Note

I've seen rock bottom up close. I've eaten the dollar-menu meals, counted pennies at the gas pump, and asked myself how much lower things could go. I've slept with anxiety gnawing at my chest, wondering if tomorrow would bring relief or just another bill I couldn't pay. At the time, it felt hopeless. I thought I was stuck. I thought that was just "life." But looking back, those moments weren't just painful - they were pivotal. Rock bottom taught me lessons I could've never learned in comfort. And those lessons became the stepping stones out of Brokeitis.

The Gift in the Pain

If you're there right now, I know it hurts. I know it feels like nobody understands. But don't miss the lessons. Rock bottom can break you, or it can build you. The choice is yours. The lesson is clear: Brokeitis may push you to rock bottom, but rock bottom doesn't have to be the end. It can be the beginning. Because once you've been there, once you've seen how bad it can get, you gain something priceless: perspective. You stop taking small wins for granted. You start valuing peace over possessions. And you realize that no matter how far you've fallen, you can rise again.

6

HOW I CURED BROKEITIS

When you're knee-deep in Brokeitis, it feels like there's no way out. Bills stack up, stress piles on, and you start thinking this is just "normal life." The sad truth? Millions of people accept that survival is all there is. But here's the good news: Brokeitis is curable. I know, because I caught it, I lived with it, and I clawed my way out of it. It didn't happen overnight. It wasn't easy. And no, I didn't win the lottery, marry into money, or discover some hidden trust fund. What I found instead was something a lot more valuable: **know-how.** And that know-how changed everything.

Step 1: Facing the Truth

The cure started the day I stopped lying to myself. For years, denial was my medicine of choice. I'd tell myself, *"I'm fine. Things will turn around soon."* But "fine" was a lie, and "soon" never came.

- I stopped pretending I was "fine."
- I stopped flexing like I had money when I didn't.
- I stopped ignoring bills and hoping they'd magically go away.

Denial is the first stage of Brokeitis - and honesty is the first step out. I remember one night, sitting in my car outside the grocery store, staring at my bank app. I had $14.32 to my name. I could've lied to myself and said, *"It's just a tough week."* But I'd been saying that for years. That night, for the first time, I admitted: *"I'm broke. I need help."* That admission was painful. But it was also the turning point.

Reader Challenge: Open your bank app. Write down the exact number you see - no rounding up, no "forgetting" about bills coming out tomorrow. Just the raw number. That's your starting point. Truth is the cure's first dose.

Step 2: Learning the Basics (That No One Taught Me)

Here's something wild: I made it through school knowing how to solve algebra equations but not how to balance a budget. Sound familiar? Nobody handed me a "Money 101" manual. I had to teach myself. And thankfully, the internet became my teacher. Free YouTube channels, blogs, podcasts, and even random Reddit threads opened my eyes. I learned things I should've known at 16, not 30:

- How to track my spending.
- How credit scores really work.
- Why saving even $5 a week mattered. • That investing wasn't just for rich people.

The first time I heard the phrase "every dollar needs a job," it blew my mind. Up until then, I thought money was like sand - it just slipped through my fingers. Suddenly, I realized I could direct it. Brokeitis thrives on ignorance - education starves it.

Reader Challenge: This week, spend 30 minutes learning one money concept you've avoided. Budgeting, credit, savings, investing - pick one. Free resources are everywhere. The point isn't to master it overnight, but to chip away at ignorance until it has no power left.

Step 3: Cutting Out the Excess

Once I knew better, I had to do better. I asked myself one question: *Do I really need all of this stuff?* Turns out, the answer was no.

- I canceled subscriptions I barely used.
- I swapped eating out for cooking at home.
- I stopped chasing trends and started chasing stability.

It wasn't glamorous, but the truth is, Brokeitis hates discipline. Every time I said "no" to something I didn't need, I was saying "yes" to freedom. mAt first, it felt like deprivation. But over time, it felt like strength. I was in control for the first time in years. One moment sticks out: I was walking past a store, tempted to buy shoes I couldn't afford. For once, instead of saying, *"I deserve this,"* I said, *"I deserve peace more."* That shift in thinking saved me far more than the $80 on those shoes.

Reader Challenge: Write down three things you've paid for in the last month that you didn't truly need. Then, commit to cutting at least one of them this month. Brokeitis loses power every time you say no.

Step 4: Side Hustling and Resourcefulness

I didn't just cut back - I found new ways to earn. And the internet made that possible. I tried everything:

- Freelancing gigs.
- Selling old clothes and gear online.
- Picking up odd jobs like driving deliveries or tutoring.

Was it glamorous? No. Did it make me rich? Definitely not. But it created momentum. And momentum is the cure's best friend. I'll never forget the first $50 I made from a side gig. It wasn't much, but it proved something powerful: *I'm not stuck.* There are ways forward, even if they're small. And small steps build into big strides.

Reader Challenge: Write down one way you could earn an extra $50 this month. Just one. Then do it. It could be selling old clothes, doing a gig, or offering a service. The point isn't the money - it's proving to yourself that you're not powerless.

Step 5: Building a New Mindset

The biggest cure wasn't financial. It was mental. I stopped thinking like a broke person and started thinking like someone who had options.

- I shifted from *"I can't afford that"* to *"How can I afford that?"*
- I stopped blaming the system entirely and took responsibility for what I could control.
- I realized that wealth wasn't just money - it was peace, choices, and security.

That shift was everything. Because here's the truth: you can give two people the same amount of money, and one will grow it while the other wastes it. The difference isn't the dollars. It's the mindset. Brokeitis wants to keep you trapped in victim thinking. The cure flips that script.

Reader Challenge: Catch yourself the next time you say, "I can't afford that." Replace it with, "How can I afford that?" Watch how your brain shifts from hopelessness to problem-solving.

The Cure Isn't Magic - It's Consistency

Curing Brokeitis didn't mean I suddenly became a millionaire. It meant I learned how to manage money instead of letting it manage me. It meant breaking cycles. It meant creating habits that built a new normal. Here's the truth: the cure doesn't happen in a week. It happens step by step, dollar by dollar, choice by choice. But every small step is proof that you don't have to live with Brokeitis forever.

My Challenge to You

If I could cure Brokeitis, so can you. Not because I'm special, but because the cure is available to anyone willing to admit, learn, and act. This book isn't about financial perfection. It's about progress. It's about taking the first step, then another, and another, until Brokeitis is a story you used to tell - not a life you're still living.

7

SOCIETY'S ROLE IN BROKEITIS

Let's get one thing straight: you didn't catch Brokeitis all on your own. Sure, your habits play a role, but society has been setting the trap for years. In fact, Brokeitis isn't just an accident - it's by design. We live in a world that runs on consumerism, greed, and comparison. And the system is happy to keep you broke as long as you stay buying. That doesn't mean you're powerless. But it does mean the game has been rigged from the start.

The Marketing Machine

From the moment you wake up, someone is selling to you. Ads tell you you're not complete without their product. Influencers flex lifestyles they don't actually own. Companies design products to break faster so you'll buy the next one. And the kicker? They're good at it. Very good. Think about the last time you bought something you didn't really need. Maybe it was that gadget the ad called "life-changing." Maybe it was that skin-care set you saw on Instagram. Maybe it was the sneakers the algorithm knew you'd drool over. You didn't buy it because you woke up thinking, *"This is essential."* You bought it because the marketing machine whispered, *"If you have this, you'll feel better. You'll be better."* It's a trap. And most of us fall for it at some point.

Reflection Prompt: When was the last time you bought something because of an ad or an influencer - even though you didn't truly need it? What was the hidden promise that pulled you in?

The Debt Industry

Banks and credit card companies love Brokeitis. Why? Because they make billions off of it.

- Overdraft fees.
- Interest charges.
- "Buy now, pay later" schemes.

They don't want you to pay off your debt fast. They want you to stay in it, paying little by little, forever. Your Brokeitis is their business model. When I first got my credit card, I thought the bank was doing me a favor. *"Here, have some money you don't actually have - on us."* But I quickly realized they weren't doing me a favor - they were setting me up for dependency. The first time I paid only the minimum balance, I thought I was being responsible. Months later, I'd paid hundreds in interest, and the balance hadn't budged. That's when it hit me: the system isn't broken. It's working exactly as designed.

Reflection Prompt: Look at your most recent bank or credit card statement. How much of what you paid actually went toward what you owe - and how much went to fees or interest?

Throwaway Culture

We live in a society that throws away what others desperately need. Clothes, food, electronics - all tossed out while someone else goes without. Instead of fixing things, we replace them. Instead of giving away extras, we trash them. And every time we do, we reinforce the mindset that "more is normal." I once knew a family who upgraded their phones every year - not because the old ones were broken, but because the new model had a better camera. Their old phones? Shoved into a drawer, forgotten. Meanwhile, their credit cards screamed under the weight of "upgrades." Throwaway culture doesn't just waste resources. It trains us to see everything - products, money, even people - as disposable. That mindset feeds Brokeitis because it makes "enough" feel like "not enough."

Comparison as a Currency

Brokeitis thrives in the age of social media. Scroll your feed and you'll see:

- Vacations you can't afford.
- Cars you don't drive.
- Lifestyles that look perfect (but are often funded by debt).

We're all competing in a race no one actually wins. And in that race, Brokeitis is the silent referee, keeping score in late payments and stress headaches. I remember scrolling one night, seeing a friend post pictures of a dream vacation. My first thought wasn't, *"Good for them."* It was, *"Why not me?"* The jealousy was instant, even though I didn't know if they'd saved for years or just maxed out a credit card. Comparison makes us forget reality. We chase images, not truths. And in that chase, we spend money we don't have to impress people we barely know.

Reflection Prompt: Think of one purchase you've made mostly because you saw someone else with it. Did it bring lasting joy - or just temporary relief?

Silence Around Money

And let's not forget one of society's biggest contributions to Brokeitis: we don't talk about money. Families avoid the subject. Schools skip teaching it. Employers barely prepare you for it. So instead, we learn about money the hard way: overdrafts, evictions, repossessions. Society trains us to be consumers, not managers. Spend first, think later. I can still remember the first time I tried to ask my parents about credit. They changed the subject. Not because they didn't care, but because they didn't know either. That silence didn't protect me. It trapped me. When money is taboo, ignorance thrives. And ignorance is Brokeitis' best friend.

Reflection Prompt: Growing up, what messages did you hear—or not hear - about money? How have those shaped your choices today?

Why This Matters

The point isn't to say it's all the system's fault. But we can't ignore that society profits from your struggle. Brokeitis isn't just personal - it's cultural. If you've ever wondered why it feels so hard to get ahead, here's why: the system was never built for you to "win." It was built for you to keep working, keep spending, and keep the cycle going. That's why curing Brokeitis isn't just about cutting back or hustling harder. It's about waking up to the ways the world is quietly conditioning you to stay broke.

The Good News

Here's the flip side: once you see the system, you can beat it.

- You can spot the marketing trap and say, *"Nah, I don't need that."*
- You can reject the throwaway mindset and learn to value what you already have.

- You can step out of the comparison race and define success on your own terms.
- You can break the silence around money by starting conversations in your family and community.

Society may set the stage for Brokeitis, but you don't have to keep playing the role. Awareness is power. Once you see the trap, you can choose not to step in it.

8

HOW TO FIGHT BROKEITIS

Brokeitis might be the #1 disease sweeping the country, but the good news is this: it's not terminal. It can be prevented. It can be cured. And unlike most diseases, you don't need a prescription - you just need **know-how.** Let's talk about how to fight it.

Step 1: Face the Numbers

You can't cure what you won't diagnose. Most of us avoid looking at our money because it's painful. Opening the bank app feels like checking your blood pressure when you already know it's high. But ignoring the truth doesn't change it.

- Write down what you owe.
- Write down what you make.
- Write down what you spend.

That's it. No excuses. No "mental math." Put it all on paper. When I finally did this, I realized I wasn't just "a little behind" - I was drowning. I'd been telling myself a story that I was "managing," but the numbers told a different story. That shock was my wake-up call.

Ignoring your numbers is like ignoring chest pain and hoping it'll just "go away." Facing the numbers is the first shot of medicine against Brokeitis.

Reflection Prompt: On a scale of 1–10, how anxious do you feel when you open your bank app? What does that number tell you about your current relationship with money?

Micro-Challenge: Tonight, write down your total income, total expenses, and total debt - no matter how ugly it looks. This is your "before" picture.

Step 2: Separate Wants From Needs

Prevention starts with one simple question: *Do I really need this?*

- Food? Yes. DoorDash five nights a week? No.
- Clothes? Yes. Designer sneakers you can't afford? No.
- A phone? Yes. The newest iPhone every year? Definitely no.

Every time you cut a "want" disguised as a "need," you weaken Brokeitis's grip. I had a lightbulb moment when I realized my $150 monthly subscription "bundle" (streaming, apps, random services) was eating the same money I claimed I "couldn't find" for savings. It wasn't that I didn't have money. It was that I was mislabeling luxuries as necessities. Brokeitis thrives on confusion. It loves when you call "wants" by the name of "needs." Fighting back means calling things what they are.

Reflection Prompt: List the last five things you bought. Which were true needs? Which were disguised wants?

Micro-Challenge: Pick one recurring expense that's really a "want." Cancel or cut it for the next 30 days. See how much lighter you feel.

Step 3: Build a Simple Budget

Don't overcomplicate it. A budget doesn't need color-coded charts and ten categories. Start with three:

1. What's coming in.
2. What's going out.
3. What's left.

If nothing is left, adjust until there is. A budget is just a mirror - it shows you the truth so you can make changes. When I started budgeting, I hated it. It felt restrictive, like someone telling me what I couldn't do. But over time, I realized a budget wasn't punishment - it was permission. It gave me clarity. It gave me control. It gave me peace of mind I hadn't felt in years.

Reflection Prompt: Do you see budgeting as a punishment or as freedom? Why?

Micro-Challenge: Track every dollar you spend for the next 7 days. Don't judge, just write it down. Awareness comes before adjustment.

Step 4: Create a Small Emergency Fund

Even $500 saved can stop Brokeitis from spiraling. Why? Because the minute a tire blows out or a bill surprises you, you won't have to turn to credit. That little cushion can mean the difference between surviving and sinking. When I built my first emergency fund, it wasn't glamorous. It meant skipping takeout, selling a few things online, and cutting back hard. But the day my car needed a repair and I had the cash ready? That was freedom. Brokeitis hates when you have options. An emergency fund is your first line of defense.

Reflection Prompt: Think of the last "unexpected" expense you had. How would it have felt if you had $500 set aside just for that?

Micro-Challenge: Open a separate savings account (online or at your bank). Put $25–$50 in it this week. Don't touch it unless it's a true emergency.

Step 5: Kill Debt, One Step at a Time

Debt is Brokeitis's best friend. Every dollar you pay in interest is a dollar you don't get to keep.

- List your debts.
- Pick the smallest one.
- Knock it out. Then move to the next.

Every win builds momentum. I used to think, *"Why bother? My debt is too big."* But paying off one small card gave me a rush. It was proof I could move forward. That momentum carried me through the bigger debts. Brokeitis thrives in hopelessness. Debt snowballing gives you hope.

Reflection Prompt: Which debt could you realistically eliminate in the next 90 days?

Micro-Challenge: This week, make an extra payment (even $20) on your smallest debt. Don't wait until "someday." Someday starts now.

Step 6: Increase Income (Even a Little)

Cutting expenses helps - but earning more cures faster. Thanks to the internet, opportunities exist everywhere.

- Freelancing.
- Selling old stuff.
- Driving for gig apps.
- Turning a hobby into side cash.

It doesn't have to make you rich. Even an extra $100 a month can be the push that gets you out of Brokeitis. I'll never forget the feeling of selling my first old guitar online. It wasn't a fortune, but it cleared a bill. It reminded me: I wasn't stuck. I had tools. I had options.

Reflection Prompt: If you had to make an extra $100 this month, what's the first thing you'd do?

Micro-Challenge: Pick one quick side hustle this week. Sell one item online. Sign up for one gig app. Test it. Momentum matters more than perfection.

Step 7: Build "Brokeitis Immunity"

The cure isn't just fixing your money once - it's building habits that protect you in the future.

- Track your money monthly.
- Save automatically.
- Avoid debt traps.
- Teach your kids what you learned.

This is how you prevent Brokeitis from coming back. Because the disease doesn't just hit your wallet - it infects your mindset. Building immunity means creating habits so strong, relapse isn't an option.

Reflection Prompt: What's one money habit you wish your parents had taught you? How can you start teaching it to yourself (or your kids) today?

Micro-Challenge: Set up one automatic transfer this week, even if it's $10. Consistency builds immunity.

Step 8: Redefine Wealth

Here's the real secret: wealth isn't just money. It's peace. It's stability. It's waking up without panic. The cure isn't about becoming rich - it's about becoming free. I used to think wealth meant driving luxury cars and wearing designer clothes. But I've learned wealth is being able to pay your bills without sweating. It's having time with your family. It's sleeping at night without debt collectors in your dreams.

Reflection Prompt: What does "wealth" mean to you beyond money? Write it down. Redefine it for yourself, not for Instagram.

The Cure Starts Small

You don't cure Brokeitis with one big decision. You cure it with a thousand small ones:

- Skipping the impulse buy.
- Cooking instead of eating out.
- Saving instead of spending.
- Choosing peace over appearances.

Little by little, you break the cycle. And before you know it, Brokeitis becomes something you used to have - not something you live with every day. The cure isn't quick, but it's worth it. And the first step can start right now.

9

THE PSYCHOLOGY OF BROKEITIS

Money isn't just math. If it were, most of us would be fine. Add up income, subtract expenses, save the difference - easy, right? But Brokeitis doesn't live on calculators. It lives in our heads. It's emotional, mental, and deeply psychological. You can have the best budgeting app, the cleanest spreadsheet, and the tightest plan - but if your brain is still wired for Brokeitis, you'll sabotage yourself every time. That's why curing Brokeitis isn't just about your bank account. It's about your mindset.

Scarcity Mindset: The Mental Trap

When you've been broke long enough, your brain rewires itself to expect lack. That's called **scarcity mindset**.

- You buy things you don't need because you're scared the chance won't come again.
- You hoard stuff "just in case" you can't afford it later.
- You stay stuck in low-paying jobs because fear of losing "something" outweighs the hope of "something better."

I'll never forget the time I bought six jars of peanut butter on sale - not because I needed six jars, but because my brain whispered, *"What if you can't afford it later?"* Months later, half of them expired. That's how scarcity works. It convinces you to grab and hold, even when it makes no sense. Scarcity mindset convinces you there's never enough - not money, not time, not opportunity. And when you believe that, you act in ways that keep Brokeitis alive.

Reflection Prompt: Think of one time you bought or hoarded something because you were scared you wouldn't get the chance again. Did it actually help, or just clutter your life?

The Stress Spiral

Money stress isn't just "in your head." It shows up in your body. Studies link financial stress to:

- Anxiety and depression.
- Sleep problems.
- High blood pressure.
- Even weakened immune systems.

Ever stayed up at 2 a.m. doing imaginary math in your head, trying to figure out if you'll make rent? That's the stress spiral. It doesn't just drain your wallet. It drains your health. During my worst Brokeitis years, I'd wake up at night with my jaw aching from grinding my teeth. My dentist told me I needed a mouthguard. What I needed was peace. Stress was stealing both my sleep and my money - because every night of lost rest made me less effective the next day.

Reflection Prompt: How does money stress show up in your body - headaches, insomnia, tension? Write down one physical symptom you've noticed.

Shame and Silence

One of Brokeitis's nastiest tricks is shame.

- You avoid calls from creditors because you don't want to explain yourself.
- You dodge social invites because you can't afford them.
- You put on a brave face and say, "I'm good," even when you're drowning.

Shame keeps you quiet. And when you're quiet, you don't ask for help. Silence is fertilizer for Brokeitis. I once skipped a close friend's birthday dinner because I couldn't afford it. Instead of admitting the truth, I lied and said I was sick. That lie hurt the friendship more than honesty ever would have. Shame silences us until relationships pay the price. The irony? Everyone else is struggling too - but since nobody talks about it, we all think we're the only ones.

Reflection Prompt: Who in your life could you talk to honestly about money? What's stopping you from opening up?

The Comparison Curse

Nothing feeds Brokeitis faster than comparison. Social media makes it worse. You scroll and see people your age with new houses, new cars, vacations in Bali - and suddenly you feel like you're behind in life. What you don't see: the credit card bills, the loans, the stress behind the smiles. Comparison convinces you you're failing, even when you're just fighting a different battle. I remember seeing a friend post pictures of a brand-new luxury SUV. My first thought? *"Man, I'm slipping. I should be doing better."* Later, I found out the car was leased to the hilt and repossessed within a year. The picture told one story. Reality told another. Comparison is poison because it shifts the focus from progress to performance. Instead of asking, *"Am I better than I was last year?"* we ask, *"Am I better than them?"* And that question keeps Brokeitis alive.

Reflection Prompt: Think about your last scroll through social media. Did it make you feel inspired or inadequate? Why?

Learned Helplessness

After enough failures, people start to believe nothing will ever change. That's called **learned helplessness**. You give up trying. You accept Brokeitis as your permanent reality. You stop budgeting because "it never works." You stop applying for better jobs because "nobody hires people like me." You stop dreaming because "what's the point?"This is the most dangerous mindset of all - because if you believe there's no cure, you'll never look for one. I remember sitting at my kitchen table with a stack of unpaid bills, thinking, *"This is my life now. Just bills and stress until I die."* That thought scared me. Because it wasn't just about money anymore - it was about identity. Learned helplessness makes you believe your condition is permanent. But here's the truth: Brokeitis isn't permanent. It's a pattern. And patterns can be broken.

Reflection Prompt: Where in your life have you stopped trying because of repeated failures? What would happen if you gave it one more attempt, this time with a new approach?

Rewiring the Mind

The good news? Your brain can heal. Just like you trained yourself into Brokeitis thinking, you can train yourself out.

- Replace *"I'll never get ahead"* with *"I'm making progress one step at a time."*
- Replace *"I can't afford this"* with *"How can I afford this without debt?"*

- Replace silence with conversations. Talk about money with friends, family, and partners.

Every thought shift is a dose of medicine. Over time, those small rewires create new behaviors - and new results. Think about it: the same way repetition taught you Brokeitis habits (overspending, avoiding, comparing), repetition can teach you freedom habits (saving, learning, talking). The brain is plastic. It bends to practice.

Reflection Prompt: Pick one negative money phrase you often repeat. Write down a healthier replacement. Practice saying it out loud for the next week.

The Heart of the Cure

Brokeitis isn't just financial. It's psychological. It lives in the stories you tell yourself, the shame you carry, the stress you hold, and the comparisons you believe. To cure it fully, you have to treat both the bank account and the brain. Because here's the truth: you can't build wealth with a broke mindset. And the good news? The same way Brokeitis infected your thoughts one small choice at a time, you can rewire your mind one healthy thought at a time.

10

THE DIGITAL HUSTLE

If Brokeitis had a mortal enemy, it would be the internet. Never before in history have people had so many ways to make money outside of a traditional 9-to-5. At the same time, never before have so many people been scammed out of their rent money chasing "fast cash." The internet is like fire: it can cook your dinner or burn down your house. The question is, how do you use it?

The Opportunity Side

For the first time ever, you don't need permission to make money. You don't need a gatekeeper, a manager, or a boss to say "you're hired." If you've got Wi-Fi and effort, the world is open to you.

- Got a skill? Sell it on Fiverr or Upwork.
- Got an opinion? Start a YouTube channel or podcast.
- Got a closet full of junk? Sell it on eBay, Poshmark, or Facebook Marketplace.
- Got time and a car? DoorDash, Uber, and Instacart are waiting.

Millions of people have taken their first steps out of Brokeitis this way. Not by winning the lottery, but by turning little pockets of time into extra income. I remember talking to a friend who started proofreading online. At first, it was just $25 here, $50 there. But over time, those small gigs turned into steady clients. What once felt like pocket change became the seed of a new career. The internet is filled with these kinds of stories. They may not make you rich overnight, but they prove you're not trapped. You've got options.

Reflection Prompt: If you had to earn an extra $100 online this month, what skill, product, or platform could you use?

Micro-Challenge: Make one attempt this week. Post one item for sale, apply for one gig, or set up one profile. The cure starts with action.

The Trap Side

But here's the flip side: the internet also feeds Brokeitis like Miracle-Gro.

- "Get rich quick" schemes that promise six figures if you just "buy the course."
- Fake gurus flexing Lamborghinis they don't own.
- Online shopping that lets you spend money you don't have 24/7.
- Social media flex culture convincing you to spend for the 'gram.

For every person who uses the internet to build income, there are ten more who use it to dig deeper into debt. I once fell for a "work from home" course that promised I'd make thousands in my first month. The sales page was slick, the testimonials glowing, the countdown timer screaming urgency. I swiped my card. And guess what? The course was garbage. Outdated videos, vague advice, no support. The only person who made money was the so-called "guru." That's the trap. The internet gives opportunities, but it also preys on desperation. When you're broke and hungry for a way out, you're more likely to believe in shortcuts.

Reflection Prompt: Have you ever bought a product, course, or subscription online that promised more than it delivered? What did it cost you - not just in money, but in trust?

The Gig Economy Gamble

Let's talk about gig apps. They can help, but they can also trap you.

- You make quick money, but burn through gas and wear out your car.
- You get cash today, but no benefits, no retirement, no safety net.
- You hustle harder and harder just to stay in the same place.

I met a driver who worked 60 hours a week for a delivery app. On paper, he was "self-employed." In reality, he was exhausted, his car was falling apart, and every dollar earned had hidden costs. He wasn't climbing out of Brokeitis - he was running on a treadmill called the gig economy. That doesn't mean these apps are useless. They can be life-savers in emergencies or stepping stones to something bigger. But if you treat them as your long-term plan, you risk trading time for money in ways that keep you stuck.

Reflection Prompt: If you're hustling in the gig economy, is it a bridge to something better - or a hamster wheel that's keeping you tired and broke?

Micro-Challenge: This week, calculate your *true* hourly rate after expenses (gas, wear and tear, fees). Is it really worth it?

The AI Advantage (and the Trap)

The newest player in the digital hustle is **Artificial Intelligence.** Depending on how you use it, AI can be your best weapon against Brokeitis - or your fastest way into false hope. On one hand, AI is a game-changer. You can:

- Use AI tools to design logos, draft resumes, or create social media posts.
- Generate product descriptions for an online store in minutes instead of hours.
- Edit videos or brainstorm content ideas with AI-powered platforms.
- Automate repetitive tasks that used to eat up your evenings.

For someone fighting Brokeitis, AI can feel like having a personal assistant who works 24/7 for free. It levels the playing field. You don't need a big budget or a big team - you just need creativity and a willingness to learn. But here's the catch: AI is not a magic button. It's a tool. If you expect it to make you rich without effort, you'll end up disappointed - or scammed. Already, the internet is full of "AI-powered" courses, programs, and get-rich quick systems that promise automatic wealth.

One man I met dumped $997 into an "AI side hustle system" that promised to create websites and run them for passive income. What he got was a generic template and zero traffic. He lost his money and his trust. That's the AI trap. The truth is this: AI won't save you from Brokeitis if you use it to chase shortcuts. But if you use it to multiply your skills, save time, and build real value, it can accelerate your cure.

Reflection Prompt: What's one area of your life or work where AI could save you time or money if you learned to use it?

Micro-Challenge: Try one free AI tool this week (for writing, design, or productivity). See if it frees up time or opens new possibilities.

Building a Real Digital Cure

The internet isn't the enemy. The way we use it is.
To make it work for you, focus on building **assets, not just income.**

- Start something that grows: a blog, a channel, a digital store.
- Learn a skill you can raise your rates on: design, writing, coding, video editing.
- Use side hustles as a bridge, not a forever home.
- Don't fall for every shiny "money-making opportunity." If it sounds too good to be true, it usually is.
- Leverage AI as a helper, not a crutch. Use it to multiply your efforts, not replace your discipline.

I once heard someone say, *"Don't use the internet to make money once. Use it to make money forever."* That stuck with me. If you're only chasing one-time gigs, you're surviving. If you're building assets - skills, audiences, products - you're planting trees that keep bearing fruit.

Reflection Prompt: What digital skill or platform could you start building this month that might still be paying you a year from now?

The Brokeitis Filter

Here's the rule of thumb: if the internet is costing you more money than it's making you, you're feeding Brokeitis. If it's creating skills, opportunities, and income streams — you're fighting it. That's the filter. Simple, but powerful. Before you click "buy" or "sign up," ask yourself: *"Does this move me closer to freedom, or deeper into Brokeitis?"*

The Future Is Digital

The cure for Brokeitis doesn't mean abandoning the digital world. It means mastering it. Because whether we like it or not, the internet is the new marketplace, the new classroom, and the new career ladder. And AI is quickly becoming its co-pilot. The people who learn how to use these tools will cure Brokeitis faster. The people who let these tools use them will stay sick. You don't have to be a tech genius. You don't need millions of followers. You just need awareness, effort, and consistency. The digital hustle is real. And it can be your bridge out of Brokeitis - if you use it wisely.

11

THE GENERATIONAL CYCLE

Here's the thing about Brokeitis: it's not just something you "catch" as an adult. Many of us were born into it. We grew up watching it, living it, and eventually repeating it. In other words, Brokeitis runs in families. It's not genetic - it's generational.

How Brokeitis Gets Passed Down

Kids don't just inherit eye color and last names. They inherit habits, beliefs, and attitudes about money.

- If you saw your parents arguing about bills, you probably link money with stress.
- If you grew up in a house where debt was normal, you probably see credit cards as "just life."
- If nobody in your family ever saved or invested, you probably never learned how.

Brokeitis is like a hand-me-down jacket: it's too small, uncomfortable, and outdated - but people keep passing it on anyway. I'll never forget visiting a friend's house as a kid. On payday, their family tradition was to go out to eat at a buffet, load up on food, and spend almost half of what had just come in. To them, that was celebration. To me, it planted a picture: *money comes, money goes.* No one ever talked about saving for later. That unspoken lesson became a quiet inheritance.

Reflection Prompt: What was the first "money lesson" you learned just by watching your family? Did it help you — or hold you back?

The Stories We Tell

Generational Brokeitis doesn't just show up in habits. It shows up in the stories families tell.

- *"We've always struggled."*
- *"Rich people are greedy."*
- *"People like us don't get ahead."*

These phrases sound harmless, but they're powerful. They plant seeds of limitation in the next generation before kids even get a chance to dream bigger. I once heard a grandmother tell her grandson, "Don't aim too high. You'll just be disappointed." She thought she was protecting him. What she was really doing was handing him a story that said, *stay small, stay safe, stay broke.* Stories create ceilings. And unless we rewrite them, we pass those ceilings down.

Micro-Challenge: Write down three "money phrases" you heard growing up. Now rewrite each one with a healthier story (e.g., "Rich people are greedy" becomes "Money reveals who you are - generous or selfish.").

When Survival Becomes Normal

For families living paycheck to paycheck, survival isn't a temporary season - it's the norm. Kids grow up thinking scarcity is just how life works. By the time they're adults, Brokeitis feels less like a disease and more like destiny.

Imagine a child who constantly hears:

- *"We'll buy it when the check comes in."*
- *"We can't afford that."*
- *"Money doesn't grow on trees."*

That child grows up with a relationship to money built on fear and lack. Even when they start earning, they repeat the cycle - not because they're careless, but because "survival mode" is all they've ever known. I once met a man who, even after landing a well-paying job, still lived like he was broke. Not in a good, disciplined way - but in a stressed, fearful way. He couldn't enjoy his money because he expected it to vanish. That's what happens when survival becomes normal.

Reflection Prompt: Growing up, was money in your household a source of security or stress? How has that shaped the way you handle it now?

Breaking the Cycle

The cure for generational Brokeitis doesn't just mean fixing your money. It means changing the family legacy.

- Start talking about money openly with your kids.
- Teach them about saving, budgeting, and giving.
- Show them what discipline looks like, not just struggle.

It's not about making them millionaires overnight. It's about giving them tools you never had. A single mother I know used to take her daughter to the grocery store with envelopes of cash. Each envelope had a label: food, cleaning, extras. She'd let her daughter help count out the money at the register. Years later, that daughter said, “I learned more about budgeting in those grocery trips than I ever did in school.” That’s cycle-breaking in action.

Micro-Challenge: If you have kids (or younger relatives), include them in one money activity this week - whether it’s counting savings, planning a grocery budget, or setting a giving goal.

Generational Wealth vs. Generational Brokeitis

You’ve probably heard the phrase “generational wealth.” That’s when families pass down assets — homes, investments, businesses - that create stability for decades. Generational Brokeitis is the opposite. It’s when families pass down debt, poor money habits, and a belief system that keeps them broke. Both are legacies. The question is: which one will you leave? Here’s a contrast:

- Family A leaves behind a paid-off house, some savings, and children who know how to manage money. That’s generational wealth.
- Family B leaves behind maxed-out credit cards, overdue bills, and kids who never saw an example of saving. That’s generational Brokeitis.

Neither outcome happens overnight. Both are the result of repeated choices.

Reflection Prompt: Which cycle do you see more clearly in your own family - generational wealth or generational Brokeitis? How can you shift the story for the next generation?

The Hard Truth

Breaking generational Brokeitis isn’t easy. You’ll feel the pull of old habits. You might even feel guilty for doing better than your parents did. That guilt is real. It whispers: *"Who are you to break free when they struggled?"* But remember this: breaking the cycle isn't betrayal - it's progress. Your parents may not have had the tools you do. But if they could hand you better, they would have. By doing better, you're honoring their sacrifices, not erasing them. When you change the story, you don't just heal yourself. You give your children, and their children, a chance at a new legacy.

The Torch Is Yours

If Brokeitis was passed to you, it's not your fault. But if you pass it on, that's on you. You can be the one who says, *"The cycle stops here."* You can be the one who hands your kids a different inheritance: not just money, but wisdom, discipline, and freedom. Imagine a future where your child looks back and says, *"My parents were the first in our family to save, invest, and build something lasting. Because of them, I started ahead instead of behind."* That's not just curing Brokeitis. That's rewriting history.

12

BROKEITIS IN THE FUTURE

If Brokeitis is the #1 disease sweeping the country today, what happens if we don't cure it? What happens if we keep ignoring the symptoms, laughing at the memes, and treating money struggles like "just how life is"? The answer is simple: **the future gets worse.** Brokeitis isn't static. Left untreated, it grows. It multiplies. It passes down from parents to children, from one generation to the next. And unless we decide to break the cycle, it will shape not only our lives but the future of entire communities.

The Widening Gap

The rich get richer. The broke stay broke. And the middle class - the group that once defined stability - gets squeezed until it disappears. Technology, automation, and artificial intelligence are replacing jobs at lightning speed. Already we see self-checkout lanes replacing cashiers, delivery apps replacing drivers, and software replacing office workers. For those who adapt, the future holds opportunity. For those who don't, the risk is slipping deeper into Brokeitis. Take the story of Marcus. He worked in manufacturing for twenty years. When automation hit his factory, he found himself without a job — and without the digital skills to compete in a changing market. Instead of retraining, he froze. Within a year, he went from stable to struggling, relying on payday loans just to survive. The system didn't pause for him. It kept moving.

That's the scary truth: **the system doesn't care.** It will keep evolving with or without us.

Reflection Prompt: What's one skill you could begin learning today that might still be valuable 10 years from now?

The Digital Mirage

In the future, social media will only magnify Brokeitis. People will flex harder. Ads will target deeper. "Buy now, pay later" will get slicker. And the illusion of wealth will become even easier to fake. The danger? More people will be broke in real life while looking rich online. Brokeitis will thrive in the gap between appearance and reality. I once scrolled past a young couple posing in front of a luxury car. They captioned it:

> ***"Dreams do come true."***

But what they didn't post was the $1,200 monthly lease payment eating them alive. On Instagram, they looked wealthy. In reality, they were one paycheck away from losing it all. That's the future Brokeitis feeds on: a digital world where image matters more than reality. Unless we learn to define wealth differently, we'll keep trading stability for likes.

Micro-Challenge: This week, post something online that reflects real wealth - peace, family, health, gratitude - instead of material flexes. Redefine success for yourself and your circle.

The Next Generation

If the cycle isn't broken, kids will inherit not just debt, but despair. They'll grow up thinking scarcity is normal, comparison is life, and debt is destiny. Imagine a 10-year-old who watches their parents argue about bills every month. By the time they're 18, they've absorbed the message: money = stress. They carry that story into their adult life, repeating the cycle without even realizing it. But if we break the cycle?

The opposite is possible. Kids can inherit savings, skills, and financial wisdom. They can inherit hope. They can start life not ten steps behind, but ten steps ahead. Think of Maya, a single mom who started showing her son how to budget with envelopes. By the time he was 15, he knew how to save half of what he earned from his part-time job. That habit became his inheritance - a different story, a different future.

Reflection Prompt: What story about money do you want the next generation to inherit from you? Write it down.

Redefining Wealth

Here's the good news: the future doesn't have to be dark. Because the cure for Brokeitis isn't just more money. It's a new definition of wealth. Wealth is not just a fat bank account or flashy possessions. True wealth is:

- Peace of mind.
- Choices.
- Time with the people you love.
- The ability to help others.
- Security that doesn't break when the world shakes.

In a world where technology, AI, and social media will only intensify the noise, this redefinition matters more than ever. Because if we keep chasing appearances, we'll keep feeding Brokeitis. But if we shift to peace, freedom, and purpose - the disease loses its power. I once asked a retired man what wealth meant to him. He didn't mention his house or his pension. He said,

> ***"Wealth is waking up without panic. It's knowing my bills are paid, my family is okay, and I have time to drink my coffee in peace."***

That's the kind of wealth Brokeitis can't touch.

Micro-Challenge: Write your own personal definition of wealth. Keep it somewhere visible. Let it guide your choices more than ads or comparisons do.

The Choice Ahead

The future of Brokeitis isn't written yet. It depends on us - what we teach, what we model, what we change. We can keep the cycle going and watch generations struggle. Or we can break it now and build something better. The difference between being broke and not? It's not luck. It's not lottery tickets. It's **know-how, discipline, and courage.** Every dollar saved, every debt killed, every conversation with your kids - those aren't just small acts. They're bricks in a new foundation. A foundation that says: *"This family doesn't live with Brokeitis anymore."*

The Final Word

Brokeitis is real. It's everywhere. But it's not forever. This book isn't just about diagnosing a problem - it's about sparking a cure. Because if you can change your habits, shift your mindset, and refuse to pass Brokeitis on, you don't just heal your own life. You heal the future. The question is: **what legacy do you want to leave behind?**

BREAKING FREE FROM BROKEITIS

If you've made it this far, you've done more than just read a book. You've faced truths that most people spend their whole lives avoiding. You've laughed at the absurdity of our struggles, and maybe even cringed at the parts that hit too close to home. That's the beauty of Brokeitis - it's funny until it isn't. Think back to the beginning of this journey. Remember the "symptoms" list? Checking your bank app like the weather. Stretching $5 worth of gas like it's an Olympic sport. Turning ramen noodles into meal prep.

Those examples made you chuckle - maybe even nod your head in recognition. But as you read further, you saw the deeper truth: behind every funny story is real stress. Behind every meme is a family living paycheck to paycheck. Behind every "I'm just broke until payday" joke is someone quietly losing sleep. And here's the message I want you to carry with you: **Brokeitis is not a life sentence.** You are not doomed to repeat the same mistakes. You are not destined to stay broke. You are not required to inherit the habits, fears, and silence that fed this disease in the first place. You have the power to rewrite the story.

Every Choice Matters

The cure doesn't come in one big moment. It comes in the hundreds of small choices you make every single day:

- Choosing to save instead of spend.
- Choosing to learn instead of ignore.
- Choosing to talk instead of stay silent.

Each of these choices is a step toward freedom. Every small win is proof that you are stronger than the cycle. Every time you model a new habit, you plant a seed for the people who come after you. I've said it before: Brokeitis thrives in silence. But you've broken that silence just by reading these pages, reflecting on your own habits, and considering a new path forward.

From Survivor to Legacy Builder

Maybe you've carried Brokeitis for years. Maybe it was passed to you through your family, through culture, through a system designed to keep you stuck. If so, it's not your fault. But what you do next? That's on you. You have a choice: pass Brokeitis on like a hand-me-down jacket, or be the one who says, *"This cycle stops with me."* Breaking free doesn't just change your life. It changes your family's story. Imagine your kids - or your nieces, nephews, students, or community — growing up with financial confidence instead of fear. Imagine them inheriting wisdom, discipline, and peace instead of debt and despair. That's the legacy you can build.

Not Everyone Has Brokeitis

Now let's be clear: not everyone suffers from Brokeitis. Some people are living free from financial struggle. Their bills are covered, their future is stable, and they're not lying awake at night wondering how to stretch $5 of gas. If that's you, celebrate it. You've worked hard, made wise choices, or maybe inherited lessons that kept you ahead. But here's the challenge: don't keep it to yourself. Because human nature can be selfish. People who've "figured it out" sometimes stay quiet, enjoying their comfort while others drown. But real wealth isn't just about what you have - it's about what you share. If you've escaped Brokeitis, you have the chance to become a teacher, a mentor, a living example that freedom is possible. Don't hoard the cure. Pass it on.

Looking Ahead

We talked in Chapter 12 about the future. The widening gap between rich and poor. The illusion of wealth magnified by social media. The rise of AI and automation. The truth is, the future will only make Brokeitis more dangerous if left unchecked. But the opposite is also true: the future can be brighter than we imagine if more people start breaking the cycle now. The cure isn't just about building bigger bank accounts. It's about redefining wealth altogether: peace of mind, choices, time with loved ones, security that doesn't shatter when the world shakes. When enough people choose this definition of wealth, Brokeitis loses its grip.

Your Next Step

This book may be ending, but your story is still being written. Tonight, tomorrow, or this week - you will face a choice. Spend or save. Ignore or learn. Hide or talk. That choice may seem small, but it's not. It's a brick in the foundation of your future. So here's my final challenge to you:

- Make one decision today your future self will thank you for.
- Start one new habit that fights Brokeitis instead of feeding it.
- Share one lesson from this book with someone you care about.

Because freedom spreads the same way Brokeitis does - person to person, conversation to conversation, habit to habit.

The Final Word

One day, I hope you'll look back and say:

> ***"Yeah, I had Brokeitis once. But I cured it. And I never let it come back."***

Because the truth is simple: Brokeitis is real. It's everywhere. But it's not forever. The cure is in your hands now. Don't waste it. Live it. Share it. Pass it on. Because the only thing stronger than Brokeitis is the choice to break it.

THE CURE IS CHOICE.

THANK YOU TO THE READER

If you've made it to this page, I want to pause and simply say:

thank you.

Thank you for trusting me with your time, your attention, and your story. Out of all the books you could've chosen, you chose this one. That means something to me - and I don't take it lightly. Writing this book wasn't just about pointing out the problem of Brokeitis. It was about reaching people like you - people willing to laugh, reflect, and most importantly, change. Every page you've read, every idea you've wrestled with, every choice you'll make moving forward - that's the real heartbeat of this book.

If something here made you think, smile, or even squirm a little, then it did its job. But more than that, my hope is that it gave you courage. Courage to face your numbers. Courage to challenge old habits. Courage to break cycles - not just for yourself, but for the people who will come after you. Because at the end of the day, this book isn't really about money. It's about freedom. It's about peace. It's about creating a future where Brokeitis is a story we used to tell, not a life we still live. So from my heart to yours: thank you. Thank you for reading. Thank you for showing up for yourself. And thank you for being part of the movement to break free. The cure is in your hands now. Use it well.

With gratitude,

Noah Wayan

REFLECTION GUIDE: BREAKING FREE FROM BROKEITIS

Reading about Brokeitis is one thing. Living free from it is another. Use these prompts to reflect, journal, or start conversations with people you trust. Your answers don't have to be perfect - they just have to be honest.

1. Facing the Truth

- Which "symptoms" of Brokeitis do you recognize in your own life?
- How has ignoring money problems hurt you in the past?
- What emotions come up when you check your bank balance - fear, shame, avoidance, hope?

2. The Root Cause

- What habits, beliefs, or family patterns have kept you stuck financially?
- Do you see yourself in any of the types of Brokeitis (paycheck-to-paycheck, debt-driven, lifestyle, generational, crisis)? Which ones?

- Which story about money have you been telling yourself that it's time to rewrite?

3. Rock Bottom Lessons

- What was your lowest financial moment? What did you learn from it?
- How did that season shape the way you view money today?
- How can you use that experience as fuel to build something better?

4. Curing Brokeitis

- What's one practical step you can take this week to fight Brokeitis (cutting an expense, starting a side hustle, building a small savings)?
- What money habit do you want to start building today that your future self will thank you for?
- Who in your life can support you or hold you accountable as you take this step?

5. Society and Comparison

- How has advertising, social media, or comparison influenced your spending?
- What traps do you fall into most often (buy now/pay later, flexing, impulse shopping, etc.)?
- What boundaries or strategies could you put in place to protect yourself from those traps?

6. Generational Change

- What money lessons did you inherit from your family?
- Which of those lessons do you want to keep — and which do you want to break?

- What financial wisdom do you want to pass down to the next generation?
- How would it feel for your kids (or future kids) to start life 10 steps ahead instead of 10 steps behind?

7. Redefining Wealth

- When you think about being "wealthy," what comes to mind?
- Beyond money, what does true wealth look like for you (peace, time, choices, security, freedom)?
- What's one change you could make today to align your life more with that definition of wealth?

Final Challenge

Imagine it's 10 years from now. Someone asks you, *"How did you cure Brokeitis?"*

- What story do you want to tell?
- What choices did you make that changed your future?
- What legacy did you leave behind?

Write that story now - and then go live it.

NEXT STEPS & RESOURCES

Breaking free from Brokeitis isn't just about reading a book - it's about taking action. Here are some next steps and resources to keep you moving forward:

1. Start Small, Start Now

Don't wait for the "perfect moment." Pick one simple step to take this week:

- Cancel one expense you don't need.
- Put $25 into a savings account.
- Track every dollar you spend for seven days.

Momentum begins with small wins.

2. Build Your Toolkit

Here are a few practical tools to help you fight Brokeitis:

- **Budgeting Apps** - YNAB (You Need a Budget), EveryDollar, or Mint can help you see where your money is really going.
- **Saving & Investing Apps** - Acorns, Stash, or Robinhood make it easier to start small.
- **Debt Payoff Calculators** - Free tools online can show you how fast you can get out of debt with extra payments.

(*Note: I don't earn from recommending these - they're simply options to explore.*)

3. Keep Learning

The cure for Brokeitis thrives on knowledge. Feed your mind with resources that will keep you sharp and inspired:

- **Books** - *The Total Money Makeover* by Dave Ramsey, *Your Money or Your Life* by Vicki Robin, *I Will Teach You to Be Rich* by Ramit Sethi.
- **Podcasts & YouTube Channels** - Choose creators who focus on practical steps, not hype. Look for voices that align with your values.
- **Communities** - Join online groups or local meetups where people talk honestly about money.

4. Share the Cure

Brokeitis thrives in silence. One of the most powerful things you can do is break that silence:

- Talk openly about money with your family and friends.
- Share one lesson from this book with someone you trust.
- Consider leading a small group or book club discussion using the Reflection Guide.

Freedom spreads person to person, conversation to conversation.

5. Stay Connected

This book is just the beginning. I'm building resources to go even deeper - including a workbook, courses, and online tools - so you can keep the momentum going.

Visit **[Your Website Here]** to:

- Access free worksheets and bonus content.
- Join an email list for encouragement and new tools.
- Stay updated on future projects that will help you keep Brokeitis from coming back.

6. Decide Your Legacy

Finally, remember: this isn't just about you. It's about what you pass down.

- Will your family inherit Brokeitis - or financial wisdom?
- Will your legacy be debt and despair - or peace and security?

The choice is yours. And it begins today.

Final Word: You have everything you need to start breaking free right now. Don't wait for someday. Someday is today.

ABOUT THE AUTHOR

Noah Wayan is a truth-teller, heart-listener, and advocate for emotional healing and personal awakening. With a voice that blends honesty, compassion, and quiet strength, his work speaks to those who are ready to live more intentionally, love more deeply, and stop sleep-walking through life.

Known for his soulful storytelling and deeply reflective style, Noah writes for those standing at a crossroads - ready to remember who they are and realign with what really matters. When he's not writing, Noah is speaking, mentoring, and walking his own path of purposeful living - one moment at a time.

ALSO BY NOAH WAYAN

All Was Good Until You…is a powerful, eye-opening exploration of how emotional immaturity - hidden behind silence, control, and unhealed wounds - quietly erodes our closest relationships across every corner of life.

Every Moment Counts…invites you to pause, reflect, and realign with what's truly important. Through soulful insights and gentle truth-telling, this book helps you step out of survival mode and into a life of intention, presence, and purpose.

I'm Ready Too!…This powerful guide shines a light on the emotional struggles men face when taught to hide their feelings. Through raw honesty and healing insights, *I'm Ready Too!* helps men break free from emotional silence, reconnect with their truth, and build deeper, healthier relationships. A must-read for any man ready to grow - and for those who love him.

The Do Book…s your wake-up call, your battle cry, your no-excuses guide to finally starting what you've been putting off. Whether it's launching that business, writing that book, going to the gym, or just making a move on a long-delayed dream - this short, sharp, and soul-stirring read will help you stop waiting and start doing.

From the Mind to the Hand…In this transformative guide, author and creative mentor Noah Wayan walks you through the sacred journey of turning inspiration into reality. From the Mind to the Hand is more than a motivational book - it's a blueprint for moving from imagination to execution with clarity, confidence, and consistency.

Made in the USA
Monee, IL
04 November 2026

67382709R10056